THE IROQUOIS

CRAIG A. DOHERTY AND KATHERINE M. DOHERTY
THE IROQUOIS

Franklin Watts   New York   London   Toronto   Sydney   A First Book   1989

Map by Joe LeMonnier
Cover photo courtesy of: Museum of the American Indian

Photographs courtesy of: Rare Book Division, New York Public Library:
p. 13; The Granger Collection: pp. 14, 20; Rochester Museum & Science
Center: pp. 19, 23, 30, 33, 39, 46, 49, 50, 53, 56, 57; Reader's
Digest: pp. 26 (Michael Herring), 41 (top, Michael Hampshire); Museum
of the American Indian: pp. 3, 29, 36, 47; British Museum: p. 35;
Colgate University, Herbert Bigford Sr. Collection: p. 38; National
Museum of Man, National Museums of Canada: 41 (bottom); Art Resource:
p. 43 (Joseph Martin/Scala); Photo Researchers: 60 (Peter Kaplan)

Library of Congress Cataloging-in-Publication Data

Doherty, Craig A.
The Iroquois / by Craig A. Doherty and Katherine M. Doherty.
p.   cm.—(A First book)
Bibliography: p.
Includes index.
Summary: Examines the history, social and political organization, religion,
customs, traditional lifestyle, and current situation of the Iroquois Indians.
ISBN 0-531-10747-7
1. Iroquois Indians—Juvenile literature.   [1. Iroquois Indians.   2. Indians
of North America.]   I. Doherty, Katherine M.   II. Title.   III. Series.
E99.I7D56 1989
970.0004'975—dc20   89-33055   CIP   AC

CONTENTS

THE IROQUOIS

INTRODUCTION

Most scientists believe that the Indians of the Americas originally came from Asia. The first Americans were big-game hunters. They hunted woolly mammoths, bison, and other large Ice Age animals. The hunters first arrived during the Ice Age. As more and more of the world's water became trapped in the glaciers of the Ice Age, the oceans receded, exposing more land. The shallow Bering Sea between Asia and North America became a land bridge over which the nomadic (wandering) hunters could walk across to North America. The first Asian hunters may have crossed the land bridge to North America fifteen to forty thousand years ago. Once they had crossed the land bridge, the hunters later spread out to parts of North, South, and Central America.

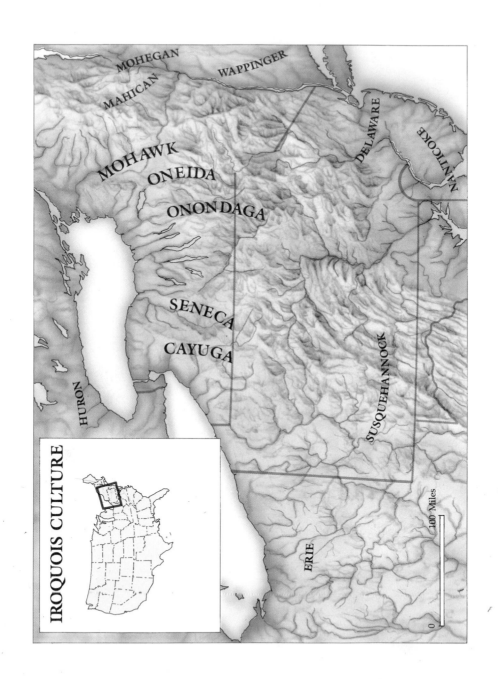

IROQUOIS CULTURE

MOHEGAN

MAHICAN

WAPPINGER

DELAWARE

NANTICOKE

MOHAWK

ONEIDA

ONONDAGA

SENECA

CAYUGA

HURON

SUSQUEHANNOCK

ERIE

100 Miles

0

IROQUOIS HISTORY

The Indians who settled in the forests of the eastern United States are known as Woodland Indians. Many different groups of Woodland Indians developed. From the Cherokee in the south to the Passamaquoddy in Maine, these Indians shared many cultural traits. One of the best known of the Woodland Indian groups is the Iroquois. For the last several thousand years, the Iroquois have lived around the lower Great Lakes in northern Ohio, Pennsylvania, and New York and further north into Canada.

Over time, the Iroquois culture developed from a hunting and gathering one to a well-developed agricultural culture. The Iroquois learned to use the forests that surrounded them as a source for many of their needs. They also adopted the agricultural plants that had developed far to the south in Central America. Corn, beans, and squash became the main food sources of the Iroquois.

The Iroquois are related through language to many other Indian groups. The Iroquoian language group includes the Cherokee, Huron, Laurentian, Susquehannock, Nottoway, and the Tuscarora. The five tribes of the Iroquois League also speak Iroquoian languages.

Historians believe that the League of the Iroquois was formed sometime between 1350 and 1600. Originally there were five tribes in the League: the Seneca, Cayuga, Onondaga, Oneida, and Mohawk. The League was formed to bring peace to these five tribes, who in the past had fought among themselves. In the early 1700s, the Tuscarora moved from the Carolinas to New York.

Legends tell that Deganawida, a Huron prophet, was sent to the Iroquois by the Creator. He traveled in a white stone canoe that convinced the Iroquois that he was sent by the Creator. His message of peace and power became the foundation of the Iroquois League. It is also said that Deganawida had a speech problem. Hiawatha, an Iroquois, not the Hiawatha of Longfellow's poem, spoke for him. Together they helped establish the Great Peace of the League.

IROQUOIS LEADERS ASSEMBLED TO RECITE
THE LAWS OF THE FIVE NATIONS
CONFEDERACY. IN THE FOREGROUND IS
AN ENLARGED VIEW OF THE WAMPUM BELT
FROM WHICH THEY "READ" THESE LAWS.

The League of the Iroquois is what is called an oligarchy. An oligarchy is a type of government that is ruled by a small group of people. The Iroquois League was ruled by fifty council members. Benjamin Franklin was so impressed by the Iroquois League that he used it as a model when helping to form aspects of the government of the newly created United States of America.

War and Warriors → The League of the Iroquois was formed to bring peace to the Five Nations of the Iroquois. The League did bring peace between the five nations, but it did not put an end to war with other neighbors. Like many other groups, warfare was an accepted fact of life for the Iroquois. The best warriors were among the most respected members of the community.

ALTHOUGH THE LEAGUE OF THE IROQUOIS BROUGHT PEACE TO THOSE NATIONS, THE IROQUOIS DID FIGHT WITH OTHER GROUPS. HERE THE IROQUOIS (RIGHT) BATTLE ANOTHER INDIAN NATION.

The Iroquois fought to protect their traditional hunting grounds. After the formation of the League, the Iroquois tried to force other tribes into accepting the code of the League. Sometimes battles were fought, or neighbors were attacked, because of long-standing rivalries. Captives were often taken. Many times, these captives were adopted. They would replace members of the captors' village who had been lost in battle.

After the Europeans began trading for furs with the various Indians of the Northeast, warfare between the tribes increased. To satisfy the European demand for furs, the Iroquois hunters traveled farther and farther. As they expanded their hunting territory, they came into conflict with other Indian groups.

The gun changed warfare for the Iroquois. They then switched from large war parties to much smaller bands. When conflicts broke out between the various European groups, the Indians would often take sides. In the French and Indian War, the Iroquois were one of the few Indian groups to assist the English. Many Iroquois stayed loyal to the English during the American Revolution. The Tuscarora and Oneida joined the colonists, whereas the Mohawk, Seneca, Cayuga, and Onondaga supported the British. After the success of the colonists, many Iroquois moved north into Canada, where they settled.

SOCIAL AND POLITICAL ORGANIZATION

Among the Iroquois, the longhouse family was the most important unit. The Iroquois lived in longhouses, which averaged 25 feet (7.6 m) by 80 feet (24.4 m) in size. Usually between thirty and sixty people lived in each longhouse. Each longhouse contained an extended family. All the people who lived in one longhouse would be related. The relations within the longhouse were matriarchal. This means that they were headed by a woman. The adult males would only be members by marriage. Within the longhouse there would be between three and five cooking fires. Each fire would be shared by two nuclear families. A nuclear family consists of a mother, a father, and their children.

The Iroquois families kept careful track of their past. Each longhouse family kept track of whom it was descended from. Each longhouse family could also trace its lineage back through a number of generations to the family's original longhouse.

In addition to its lineage, each longhouse family also belonged to a clan. Each clan was made up of longhouse families that claimed descent from a common ancestor. The clans were named after the animals of the forests. At one time it is believed that there were eight clans represented by the wolf, bear, beaver, turtle, deer, snipe, heron, and hawk. Members of a clan were thought of as siblings, brothers and sisters, within their own tribe and within the confederacy. Children always became members of their mother's clan, rather than their father's clan.

Within each tribe the members were divided into half-tribes or moieties. The two moieties would assist each other with religious ceremonies and would compete against each other in games.

Each tribe had a number of villages. Iroquois villages were usually built on high ground near a source of drinking water. The villages were often near a stream, river, or lake that could be used for travel by canoe. The population of Iroquois villages ranged from as few as fifty to as many as one thousand people. Each village was run by a council.

At the top of the Iroquois social organization was the League council, which consisted of fifty members. Each tribe had a set number of members on the council: the Mohawk and Oneida each had nine, the Onondaga had fourteen, the Cayuga had ten, and the Seneca had eight. These council members were called sachems.

Sachemships were hereditary within family lineages. The head mother with the help of the other women in her family lineage would choose the sachem. These women could also remove a sachem from the council if they were unhappy with his actions. The sachem would take the name of the original sachem elected by his family lineage.

In addition to the sachems, there were special council members called Pine Trees. Pine Trees were men and women of the tribes who had distinguished themselves in some way. Often they were famous warriors. The Pine Trees were allowed to speak at council meetings, but only sachems were allowed to vote. The council's main duty was to keep the peace among the tribes of the confederacy.

The confederacy saw itself as uniting the five tribes into one longhouse family. The Iroquois referred to themselves collectively as the People of the Longhouse.

MEMBERS OF THE COUNCIL WHEN
THE LEAGUE WAS STARTED

Wampum → Wampum was very valuable to the Iroquois. It was presented as a gift at important councils. When the Europeans came to understand the importance of wampum, they began to manufacture it. Wampum factories were built on Long Island, New York, and in New Jersey. The Europeans then used it as an item of trade. For example, they traded wampum with the Iroquois for furs.

AN IROQUOIS
WAMPUM BELT

Wampum beads were made from seashells. Two colors of wampum beads were used: white and purple. The white beads could be made from a variety of shells. The purple beads could only be made from quahog clam shells. The Iroquois would travel great distances to trade for shells and wampum with the coastal Indians. Once they got the shells, it was hard work for the Iroquois to make the beads. Each bead had to be shaped by hand and then drilled with certain tools. Many of the beads used by the Iroquois were made by other groups. The wampum would then be strung in a variety of ways.

Using the two colors, the Iroquois wove belts or strips of wampum. They would create a design that would help people remember important events. Wampum belts were also made to symbolize treaties between the Iroquois and between the Iroquois and their neighbors. They also used strings of wampum to identify Iroquois messengers. Wampum is something that developed at about the same time that the Iroquois formed the League. Many people give Hiawatha, the organizer of the League, credit for inventing wampum.

RELIGION, BELIEFS, AND CUSTOMS

All cultures have their own version of where their people came from. Many Christians believe that the first people on earth were Adam and Eve in the Garden of Eden. It is the traditional Iroquois belief that their world was created by Sky Woman.

Sky Woman was the wife of the ancient chief of the Sky World. In the center of the Sky World stood the most beautiful tree. This tree became uprooted, and Sky Woman fell through the hole where the tree had grown. The earth below was completely covered by water. Swans flew up and caught Sky Woman after she fell through the hole. A giant turtle came up from the depths. The swans placed Sky Woman safely on the turtle's back. Other animals brought up mud from

THE IROQUOIS BELIEVED THAT SKY WOMAN CREATED
THE WORLD. HER "GRANDSONS" WERE THOUGHT
TO BE RESPONSIBLE FOR THE GOOD AND EVIL IN THE
WORLD: THE "GOOD BROTHER" FOR ALL THAT WAS
GOOD, THE "EVIL BROTHER" FOR WHAT WAS BAD

the bottom that they placed on the turtle's back. The mud became the land, and the land became larger.

Sky Woman brought seeds with her and gave the world plants. Over time she gave birth to a daughter. Sky Woman's daughter gave birth to the Two Brothers. The Two Brothers created the rest of the Iroquois world. The Good Brother created all the good things, and the Evil Brother is responsible for all that is bad in the world.

For the Iroquois, their religious beliefs and daily lives are closely related. Every part of their lives is touched by their religion. The Iroquois believe in a Creator, or Master of Life, who is called, in the Seneca language, Ha-wen-ne-yu. The Creator has an evil twin brother called Ha-ne-go-ate-geh. If the Iroquois do not conduct themselves in the proper way, the Evil Brother will gain the upper hand.

The Iroquois also believe in a thunder god called He-no. He-no was in charge of rain, clouds, and thunder. It is believed that he once lived in a cave behind Niagara Falls. The Iroquois believe in many other supernatural beings.

The Three Sisters, the spirits of corn, beans, and squash, are very important. Thanks is given to them at every meal. They are referred to as De-o-ha-ko, our supporters. Each plant and animal species has its own spirit.

FALSE FACE SOCIETY MEMBERS, THEIR FEATURES
HIDDEN BY CARVED MASKS, PRACTICE THEIR HEALING
RITUALS ON AN IROQUOIS TRIBESMAN SUFFERING
FROM A SEVERE HEADACHE. THE BRIEF CEREMONY
TAKES PLACE IN THE LONGHOUSE, WHICH NO ONE
IS ALLOWED TO ENTER DURING THE RITUAL.

The Iroquois had six main religious observances during the year. The first ceremony was the Iroquois New Year celebration. This came at midwinter and symbolized the beginning of the next cycle in the life of the Iroquois. The celebration lasted for seven days.

The next important event in the Iroquois year was the Maple Dance. This was held when the maple sap began to run, usually in late February or early March each year. The purpose of this dance was to give thanks to the maple for its sap and to the Creator for giving the Iroquois the maple. This ceremony lasted for one day.

In late May or early June, the Iroquois held their Planting Festival to mark the beginning of the planting season. The Iroquois would ask the Three Sisters for their aid in growing a successful crop. They also gave thanks to the Creator. This was another one-day festival.

The next celebration, the Strawberry Festival, came when the first berries began to ripen in June. The Strawberry Festival lasted one day during which the Iroquois gave thanks to the strawberry spirit for its berries. They also gave thanks to the Creator for providing them with the strawberry.

The Green Corn Festival came next. This festival, which lasted four days, came when the corn, beans, and squash were first ripe enough to eat. Thanks was given to the Three Sisters for their help in the successful growth of crops.

The last ceremony of the year, the Harvest Festival, is one that is shared by many cultures. This is the most important time of thanksgiving. A successful harvest means prosperity for the coming year. The Iroquois thanksgiving lasted four days. Thanks was given to the Three Sisters and all the other spirits for their help in aiding the Iroquois people.

Another aspect of the Iroquois religion is their medicine societies. The Society of Faces or False Faces is the best known of these societies. The members of the Society of Faces fashion masks that are said to represent creatures seen in dreams. The False Faces participate in the Winter Festival. At other times during the year, they are called upon to cure individuals or drive disease out of houses. The False Faces, as well as other medicine societies, are still active among the Iroquois.

DAILY LIFE

For the Iroquois, life centered around the longhouse and the village. The Iroquois depended on the forest for many things. They hunted many of the forest animals for food and skins. The growing of the Three Sisters—corn, beans, and squash—was another important aspect of the daily life of the Iroquois. The Iroquois were also well known for their skill as warriors.

Childhood ➤ The Iroquois valued their children. The children received love and attention from their parents and from the other residents of their longhouse.

When an Iroquois baby was about to be born, the mother and some of the women of her longhouse moved into a hut, where the baby was born. When the baby was a few days old, mother and child would return to the longhouse. At birth a baby would be given a name that belonged to the clan. No other living Iroquois would have the same name. At certain points later in time the child would receive new names.

The Iroquois, like many other Indians, used cradleboards for their babies. The Iroquois wrapped the newborn baby in skins, and they used dried moss as diapers. The Iroquois babies were then strapped to their cradleboards.

AN ELABORATELY
CARVED CRADLEBOARD

The Iroquois cradleboards were highly decorated. The child's clan symbol was often included in the decorative carving. The cradleboards are about fourteen inches (35 cm) wide and twenty-four inches (60 cm) long. They have a hoop that encircles the baby's face. The hoop protects the baby's head and is used to support a cover. The cover can protect the baby from insects and the weather.

Mothers carried their cradleboards by using a burden strap. The burden strap was placed around the mother's forehead and supported the cradleboard on her back. When the mother was working, she would often hang the cradleboard nearby. Babies would remain quiet and happy for hours on their cradleboards.

In the past, the Iroquois did not have schools as we know them today. However, the education of the children was very important. Many people shared in teaching the children. Much of what the children needed to learn they learned through watching adults. The only formal instruction that children received was about their religion. The girls were encouraged to work alongside their mothers. As soon as they could, the girls began helping with the household chores. The responsibility for educating young boys often fell to their fathers and uncles. The boys had to learn the many skills they would need to become good hunters and warriors.

During the winter months, all the Iroquois children would be taught by the elders of the longhouse. The elders would tell stories that were intended to instruct the listeners in the proper way of behaving. Other stories might deal with the history or religion of the Iroquois. Stories were not told in the summer because the children were informed that the animals of the forest would stop to listen to the stories. If they stopped to listen, the animals would not get their work done; that is, the bees would not make honey, beavers would not build their dams, and so on.

Iroquois children who misbehaved were told stories that showed the correct way to behave. If after listening to several stories, a child continued to misbehave, he or she would be dealt with more harshly. Sometimes a child would be disciplined by being sent out of the longhouse at night. Outside, an adult would be waiting, wearing a scary mask. The adult would try to scare the child into acting correctly.

One of the first and most important things all Iroquois children were taught was to respect their elders. This is still true today. Many children who go off to school during the day come home and receive a traditional education from their elders.

Shelter ➙ Many items that the Iroquois used were made from the bark and wood of the elm tree. Foremost among these was the longhouse. The longhouses and other items made from bark were usually made in the late spring to early summer. At that time the bark of the elm peeled easily from the trees, making it easier to work with.

The longhouse was constructed using a framework of poles that were lashed together. The Iroquois built longhouses with rounded roofs. After the Europeans arrived, some Iroquois longhouses were built copying the straight walls and pitched roofs of the Europeans. Over this frame they placed overlapping sheets of elm bark. Another frame was placed over the bark to hold it in place. Doors were placed at either end of the longhouse.

A LONGHOUSE UNDER CONSTRUCTION. LONGHOUSES
WERE THE CENTRAL ELEMENT OF AN IROQUOIS
VILLAGE. THEY WERE MADE OF BARK AND WOOD AND
SOME HOUSED AS MANY AS TWENTY FAMILIES.

Longhouses varied considerably in size. The smaller ones ·were 12 feet (3.7 m) by about 30 feet (9.1 m). Some of the largest were 25 feet (7.6 m) by 200 feet (60.8 m). On average, an Iroquois longhouse was 25 feet (7.6 m) by about 80 feet (24.4 m).

Each longhouse was divided into apartments. A central corridor ran down the center of the longhouse. Partitions for the apartments were built from 12 feet (3.7 m) to 25 feet (7.6 m) apart. Each section contained two families, one on either side of the corridor.

A cooking fire was kept in the center of the section. Each fire was shared by the two families. The typical longhouse had between three and five fires. The largest longhouses might have as many as ten fires and twenty families.

Within each apartment, platforms were built. The platforms were about 1 foot (37 m) high. This kept people off the damp floor. The platforms were covered with woven reed mats or furs. During the day, people sat on the platforms. At night, the platforms were used for sleeping. Above the platforms the Iroquois built storage shelves. Between the apartments they left a storage area for food.

The Iroquois also fortified their villages. They dug a trench around a village. The area of the village might be as large as five (2 ha) to ten acres (4 ha). The trench was about 3 feet (1 m) deep. The dirt from the trench was piled on the village side of the trench. The Iroquois then put a continuous row of stakes in the mound of dirt. The stakes leaned out over the trench. This row of stakes is called a palisade. Sometimes the village had as many as three such palisades. Inside the palisade were the longhouses and the Iroquois' food stores. Outside the palisade were the fields of the village. As the strength of the League brought more peaceful times to the Iroquois, the practice of fortifying their villages lessened.

A TYPICAL IROQUOIS VILLAGE,
WELL FORTIFIED

THE IROQUOIS DYED DEERHIDE AND OFTEN
DECORATED IT FOR ARTICLES OF CLOTHING.

Clothing ➤ Prior to the coming of the Europeans,
the Iroquois made all their clothes from the skins of
animals. The skin of the deer, called buckskin, was used
the most. Frequently the Iroquois dyed the buckskin
black. The winter and summer outfits were different.
In summer, the women wore buckskin skirts and leggings. Men wore kilts or breechcloths.

In the winter, the women wore buckskin dresses,
leggings, and moccasins. The men wore buckskin leg-

gings, breechcloths or kilts, shirts, and moccasins. The men also wore caps. Their caps were built with a framework that made the crown of the cap look a little like a derby. Feathers were attached to the back of the cap. An eagle plume was the favorite type of feather used. Both men and women used furs in the winter to keep warm. The Iroquois often decorated their clothing.

Porcupine quills, moose hair, and other natural items were used for decoration before the Europeans came. The Europeans introduced the Iroquois to woven textiles. The Iroquois used the European cloth, but continued to use their traditional style of dress. The Europeans also introduced a variety of trade beads, buttons, and ribbons to the Iroquois. The Iroquois added these European beads and other finery to the decorations on their clothes.

In addition to the decorations on their clothing, the Iroquois men decorated their bodies. At one time, tattooing was common among the Iroquois men. Various geometric designs were often used. Many men had tattoos that represented their clan symbols. The tattoos were scratched or picked using a bone awl. Then charcoal was rubbed into the wound.

Iroquois women were partial to jewelry. Prior to European contact, they used the teeth of animals and shells to make jewelry. Sometimes they made necklaces of fragrant grasses. After European trade silver became available to Iroquois women, they began to wear many silver items. Earrings, rings, necklaces, broaches, buttons, hatbands, beads, and crosses all made of silver found their way onto the outfit of the well-dressed Iroquois woman. The Iroquois became so partial to trade silver that they learned how to make their own silver items.

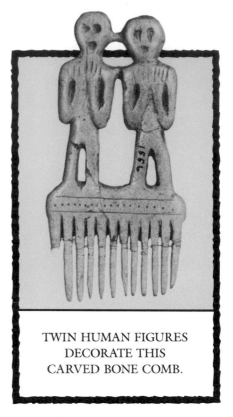

TWIN HUMAN FIGURES
DECORATE THIS
CARVED BONE COMB.

The Iroquois were also excellent moccasin makers. Different groups had different styles of moccasins. Generally, the moccasins were made from a single piece of buckskin and were seamed over the toes and at the heel. Quills and beads were fashioned into a design over the toes. The moccasins had flaps that could be worn up on the ankles and tied with buckskin laces, although it was more likely that an Iroquois would wear the flaps down. The flaps were usually decorated with bead and quill work. In the summer, the Iroquois often wore cooler slippers that were made of corn husks.

Games ➜ The Iroquois played a wide variety of games. Some of these games are still played. The best known of all the Iroquois games is lacrosse. Lacrosse is still played today in many high schools and colleges. The Iroquois also still play lacrosse and have sent teams to many international tournaments.

Lacrosse is a game played with a hard ball. The first Iroquois lacrosse balls were made of wood. Originally, the Iroquois used a solid stick, but they eventually developed the style of lacrosse stick that is still

LACROSSE IS THE BEST KNOWN IROQUOIS GAME. IT IS STILL PLAYED IN HIGH SCHOOLS AND COLLEGES AROUND THE COUNTRY.

in use today. Iroquois living in Canada make many of the lacrosse sticks used today.

The Iroquois played lacrosse with six to eight players on a side. Teams were drawn from the moieties within the village. Villages also competed against other villages. Sometimes nations competed against other nations. Legends claim that one lacrosse game between the Seneca and the Erie resulted in a war between the two tribes.

The Iroquois played many other games. Snowsnake was a game that entertained the Iroquois in the winter. To play snowsnake the Iroquois first made a long, narrow track in the snow. The track was sprinkled with water, creating a slick, frozen track for the snowsnake to travel in. The snowsnakes were made of wood and varied in design. Everyone had his or her own idea about how long or short to make the snake. Often the snakes would have weighted tips. To play snowsnake the Iroquois stood at the end of the track and slid the snake up the track. The person who could make the snake slide the farthest was the winner. Snowsnake was usually played by the younger members of the village.

The Iroquois games were often played as part of their religious festivals. They had many different games to test the athletic skills of the young men. The Iroquois also liked to play a variety of games of chance.

ABOVE: SNOWSNAKE
WAS ANOTHER IROQUOIS
GAME. IT REQUIRED CON-
SIDERABLE STRENGTH AND
SKILL. RIGHT: A LESS
STRENUOUS IROQUOIS GAME
CONSISTED OF A DECORATED
WOODEN BOWL CONTAINING
SIX PEACH PITS, ONE SIDE
OF EACH CHARRED BLACK,
THE OTHER WHITE. THE
OBJECT OF THE GAME,
PLAYED BY TWO COMPETING TEAMS, WAS TO RAP THE
BOWL SHARPLY AGAINST THE GROUND AND IF FIVE OR
SIX PITS TURNED UP THE SAME COLOR THAT PERSON
SCORED AND WENT AGAIN. IF NOT, SOMEONE ON THE
OPPOSING TEAM TOOK HIS OR HER TURN.

Transportation ➤ The territory of the Iroquois extended over many hundreds of miles. The main form of transportation for them was on foot. Established trails crisscrossed the Iroquois homelands. The warriors and hunters of the Iroquois prided themselves on their ability to cover great distances quickly. This tradition has been carried on into modern times by famous Iroquois long-distance runners. Even the snows of winter wouldn't stop the Iroquois travelers.

When the snow was deep, the Iroquois put on their snowshoes and continued to travel. Anyone who has seen or used modern snowshoes would recognize an Iroquois snowshoe. The Iroquois snowshoe is almost identical to the snowshoe used today. It was about 3 feet (1 m) long and 16 (40 cm) inches wide. The snowshoe was made using a frame of hickory with deerskin webbing. The Iroquois claimed they could travel faster on snowshoes than they could on bare ground on foot. Hunters would regularly travel as far as 50 (80 km) miles a day on their snowshoes over the Iroquois trails.

The Central Trail of the Iroquois connected the Five Nations of the League. It began among the Mohawk villages on the Hudson River near what is now Albany, New York. The Central Trail then headed west through the villages of the Oneida, the Onondaga, and the Cayuga and ended at the western boundary of the

WEARING SNOWSHOES, THESE WARRIORS
DO THE SNOW-SHOE DANCE TO THANK
THE GREAT SPIRIT FOR THE FIRST SNOW.

Seneca lands. The trail ended on the shore of Lake Erie near the mouth of Buffalo Creek, where the city of Buffalo, New York, now stands.

In addition to foot travel, the Iroquois also used canoes. The Iroquois lived out of the range of the white birch tree that was used to make canoes in other parts of the Northeast. The Iroquois used elm or hickory bark to make canoes. Elm and hickory are not as good as birch, but they still make a very usable canoe. The Iroquois built canoes ranging in size from a one-man 12-footer (3.7 m) to a 40-footer (12.2 m) that could carry thirty men. Canoes were used extensively in the fur trade. They were also used to transport warriors. The Iroquois traveled great distances along the rivers and lakes of their region in search of fur-bearing animals. The pelts were traded to the Dutch, French, and English.

FOOD

Long ago the Iroquois' ancestors were hunters and gatherers. They did not practice agriculture. All they needed to sustain life was gotten from wild plants and animals.

Corn was domesticated in Central America six thousand to eight thousand years ago and then spread throughout the Americas. It seems to have reached the Iroquois prior to one thousand years ago. Corn, along with squash and beans, soon became the mainstay of the Iroquois. From the Iroquois fields came fifteen different varieties of corn, sixty varieties of beans, and about eight different kinds of squashes. The people also grew "Indian tobacco" for ceremonial and social smoking. They used it as a medicinal plant too.

CORN WAS ONE OF THE THREE MOST IMPORTANT
CROPS TO THE IROQUOIS. THE MEN CLEARED
THE LAND; THE WOMEN DID THE PLANTING.

The Iroquois interplanted their crops. Corn, beans, and squash would all be grown in the same field. The Iroquois used a technique called slash and burn to create land for agricultural use. They cleared and then burned an area they wanted to use to plant crops. The crops were then planted on the hills between the tree stumps. Every twelve to fifteen years, the Iroquois would have to move because the fields would wear out and firewood would become scarce. The Iroquois planned ahead for these moves so they could move gradually.

Before planting, the seeds were soaked for a few days in medicine water. The medicine was said to keep away the crows. After soaking, the seeds were blessed. The men did the heavy work of clearing the land. Groups of women would do the planting. The women used hoes made of wood and bone.

During the summer, the women tended their fields. Children were stationed in tree huts in the fields. It was their job to keep away crows and other birds that might harm the crops.

CORN HUSK DOLLS ARE STILL MADE BY THE IROQUOIS TODAY, JUST AS THEY WERE YEARS AGO.

The Iroquois were very successful farmers. In most years they were able to grow an abundance of food. Corn was the main crop grown for storage. It was not unusual for the Iroquois to have a surplus of corn. The Iroquois also used the corn husks. In the summer, they made slippers out of corn husks. Dolls were also fashioned using corn husks. Some Iroquois still make corn-husk dolls.

The Iroquois built storage pits for their corn. The pits were dug, lined with bark, and then filled with corn. A watertight bark top was placed over the corn. The whole pit was then covered with dirt. The corn would keep a long time stored like this. Meat was also stored in this way. For meat, the hole was lined with deerskins.

Food Preparation ➜ Most Iroquois meals included corn. The most common dish served by the Iroquois was corn soup. Corn soup had a variety of ingredients, with corn always being the main one. The corn soup often included meat brought home by the hunters. Prior to the introduction of metal implements by the Europeans, the Iroquois cooked in pottery and wooden cookware. Food that was cooked in wooden bowls or pots was heated by putting hot stones from the fire into the bowl.

The Iroquois also made other dishes. They made a form of cornbread. They also dried and parched corn so that it could be taken on hunting trips. The Iroquois brewed many different teas from various wild plants. Meat and fish also played an important part in the diet of the Iroquois.

Hunting, Fishing, and Gathering ➜ The Iroquois claimed a vast territory as their hunting grounds. Their

HUNTING WAS IMPORTANT TO THE IROQUOIS.
THE BEST HUNTERS WERE RESPECTED AND ADMIRED
BY THE OTHERS IN THE COMMUNITY.

villages were located in what is now central New York
state. They hunted throughout what is now New York,
northern Pennsylvania, Vermont, and Ohio and north
into the Canadian province of Ontario. Being a good
hunter was important to the Iroquois. The best hunters were among the most respected men in the tribe.
As the Iroquois grew in numbers, they depleted the
game that lived close to their villages. The Iroquois
were forced to travel farther away to find the deer,
bears, and small mammals that they ate.

WOMEN CONTRIBUTED TO HUNTING BY SMOKING
THE MEAT THAT WAS BROUGHT BACK TO CAMP.
HERE VENISON IS BEING SMOKED.

The Iroquois did most of their hunting during the fall and winter after the crops were harvested and stored. In the winter, the Iroquois hunters traveled on snowshoes in search of the deer yards. The snowshoe allowed the hunters to travel easily, even over the deepest snow.

The Iroquois set up hunting camps where they stayed until the middle of the winter. Women also joined the men at the hunting camp, where they assisted in preserving the bounty of the hunt. The women also took care of the camp. At hunting camp, the women dried and smoked the meat, making it into jerky. The hunters stayed in camp until it was time for the Winter Festival. By observing the Pleiades, a constellation, the hunters could tell when it was time to return to their villages.

Shortly after the Maple Festival, the spring migrations of birds began. Millions of passenger pigeons passed overhead. When the pigeons nested in the beech trees, the Iroquois caught them in nets. The baby pigeons, called squab, were poked out of the nests. The oil was extracted from the squab and then the meat was packed in bark containers. The Iroquois also hunted many other birds, including grouse, turkeys, ducks, and geese.

The primary hunting instrument of the Iroquois was the bow and arrow. In addition to the bow, the Iroquois also used a variety of snares, traps, and blow guns. Once the Europeans arrived, the Iroquois rapidly switched over to metal tools, iron traps, and guns.

In addition to eating a variety of birds and mammals, the Iroquois caught and ate a wide variety of fish and other aquatic species. Salmon, trout, bass, perch, pike, and eels were among the fish harvested from the waters by the Iroquois. Freshwater clams were a favorite of the people. The Iroquois built their villages near the many lakes and rivers of central New

York. They used the waterways for travel and also as a source of food. The Iroquois used hooks, spears, and nets to catch fish.

Family groups went to special fishing stations during the spring spawning runs. Salmon swam up the Hudson and the Iroquois caught them by the hundreds at the mouth of the Mohawk River. Other fish ran out of the lakes into smaller rivers and streams. Often the Iroquois built stone weirs to divert the fish into their nets. A weir is a series of stone walls built in a river or stream that forces the fish to swim into the fishermen's nets.

The Iroquois took full advantage of all the forest had to offer. In the spring, the Iroquois began the gathering season by collecting the sap from the maple trees. They boiled the sap down, making maple syrup and maple sugar. The first greens to come up in the forest in the spring found their way into the Iroquois cooking pots. Wild onions, skunk cabbage, milkweed, and many other plants were gathered by the Iroquois.

As the spring season progressed, the berries ripened. Strawberries, huckleberries, blackberries, raspberries, and other berries were picked by the Iroquois. Berries were eaten fresh. They were also dried on bark trays in the sun. The dried berries could then be stored to be eaten in the winter, when they were often added to bread.

IN ADDITION TO HUNTING, THE IROQUOIS GATHERED A VARIETY OF BERRIES, PLANTS, AND NUTS.

CHESTNUTS, ALONG WITH OTHER TYPES OF NUTS, WERE USED BOTH AS FOOD AND AS A SOURCE OF OIL.

The Iroquois also gathered a type of wild potato called the groundnut. They collected a variety of other roots as well. In the fall, the Iroquois women and children collected nuts—acorns, beechnuts, walnuts, hickory nuts, and chestnuts. The nuts were used as food and as a source of oil. The Iroquois also gathered many other plants they used for food, teas, and medicines.

TOOLS AND WEAPONS

The forest didn't just provide the Iroquois with a source of food. It also supplied the materials for many of the tools that the Iroquois made and used. When the Iroquois woman prepared meals for her family, she had a wide variety of bowls, dishes, spoons, and baskets that she could use. Most of the utensils found in an Iroquois longhouse were made from the wood and bark of trees. Among the trees of the forest, the elm was the most important to the Iroquois.

The Iroquois formed many things out of the bark of trees. Bark was the material used by the Iroquois to make things from houses and boats to barrels and bowls. Around the cooking fires of the Iroquois long-house, most items found were made of bark. The Iroquois also wove baskets out of cornhusks and other plants. The Europeans taught the Iroquois how to make baskets using strips of wood called splints. The Iroquois were accomplished basket makers and still make them today.

The Iroquois also made pottery. Often they would make a pot by wrapping coils of clay around a gourd. The gourd gave the pot its shape. The clay was smoothed into the desired shape. Then it was fired in hot coals. During the firing, the gourd burned away. Generally, the Iroquois pots had a rounded bottom and a square rim. The Iroquois also made tobacco pipes out of clay.

Smoking tobacco was an important part of Iroquois religious and ceremonial life. Their pipes were often decorated with birds, snakes, animals, and sometimes human faces. The prayers of the Iroquois were sent up to the Creator with the smoke from the pipe.

The Iroquois were also accomplished rope makers. Using the fibers of various barks and other plants, they made rope for fishing nets and burden straps or tumplines. Some of the burden straps were decorated with porcupine quills. The Iroquois also used rope to bind their houses together.

The Iroquois used a variety of stone tools. The stone for tools was a highly valued item. Today scientists can tell where the stone for a particular tool

THE IROQUOIS MADE POTTERY
AS WELL AS WOVE BASKETS.

came from. Flint, jasper, and chert from specific spots in and around the Iroquois' territory have been identified by archaeologists. Knives, chisels, axe heads, scrapers, spear points, and arrowheads were all made from these stones.

Stone tools were made by chipping pieces off a larger stone. Using a pointed bone, antler, or other stone, the Iroquois could quickly make a number of tools. Once the right shape for the tool was made, smaller chips would be broken off to form the sharp edge. Stone tools were very sharp and worked well.

Among the Iroquois, the bow and arrow was the most important hunting weapon. Much care was taken in making the bow and arrows. They made different types of arrowheads for use in hunting different types of animals. The Iroquois also used blow guns when

THE BOW AND ARROW WAS THE MAIN HUNTING
WEAPON OF THE IROQUOIS. BOW AND
ARROW MAKERS WERE SKILLED CRAFTSMEN.

they hunted smaller animals such as squirrels and small birds.

The Iroquois frequently fought with other tribes of the Northeast. Before the introduction of the gun, the Iroquois fought with their bows and spears. The weapon they used most in these battles was the war club. There were two different types of war clubs.

One club was made of ironwood, dense, heavy wood. The war clubs were about 2 feet (60 cm) long with a knot on the end. The knot would be carved into a ball that was 5 to 6 inches (13 to 15 cm) in diameter. The other club was the deer-horn war club. The deer-horn club was approximately 2 feet (60 cm) long. It was made of hard wood and had a 4-inch (10 cm) prong of deer antler that pointed down from the end of the club. Both styles of club were decorated with feathers. They were often ornately carved and painted. The men wore their clubs in their belts.

The early Dutch settlers traded with the Iroquois for furs. In exchange for the furs, the Dutch began giving the Iroquois guns. In a very short period of time, the Iroquois all but gave up their bows and arrows. Stone tools were replaced by metal ones. Sheffield knives replaced stone, and metal-headed tomahawks replaced their stone axes. The first iron and brass kettles that the Iroquois received from the Europeans were reworked into arrowheads and other tools.

THE IROQUOIS TODAY

Today approximately eighty thousand Iroquois live in the United States and Canada. There are eight Iroquois reservations in New York state, five Iroquois reserves in Ontario and Quebec, and one Iroquois reservation in Wisconsin. Some Iroquois live in Oklahoma. Many Iroquois have left the reservations and live in cities in the United States and Canada. The population of the Iroquois is equally split between the United States and Canada, with approximately forty thousand Iroquois living in each country.

Like many other American Indian groups, the Iroquois are experiencing an increase in interest in their traditional ways. On some reservations the Iroquois have set up their own schools. These combine the

TODAY'S IROQUOIS COMBINE MODERN
WAYS WITH THE MORE TRADITIONAL VALUES
AND BELIEFS OF THEIR CULTURE. SMOKING
A PEACE PIPE IS AN OLD TRADITION.

teaching of traditional Iroquois values with the curriculum taught in other schools throughout the United States. Many Iroquois today make a living from re-creating traditional crafts and doing other types of fine arts.

Among the Iroquois today, the League is still important. Longhouses are built today using modern materials and are used for governmental meetings. Many Iroquois still practice their traditional religion.

FOR FURTHER READING

Arden, Harvey. "The Fire That Never Dies." *National Geographic,* vol. 172, no. 3 (September 1987): 307–403.

Bierhorst, John, ed. *The Naked Bear: Folktales of the Iroquois.* New York: William Morrow, 1987.

Bjorklund, Karna L. *The Indians of Northeastern America.* New York: Dodd, Mead & Co., 1969.

Bruchac, Joseph. *Iroquois Stories: Heros and Heroines, Monsters and Magic.* Trumansburg, N.Y.: Crossing Press, 1985.

D'Amato, Janet, and Alex D'Amato. *Algonquin and Iroquois Crafts for You to Make.* New York: Julian Messner, 1979.

Hertzberg, Hazel. *The Great Tree and the Longhouse: The Culture of the Iroquois.* New York: Macmillan Co., 1966.

Johansen, Bruce E. *Forgotten Founders: Benjamin Franklin, the Iroquois and the Rationale for the American Revolution.* Ipswich, Mass.: Gambit, 1982.

Johansen, Christina B., and John P. Ferguson, eds. *Iroquois Arts, A Directory of a People and Their Work.* Warnersville, N.Y.: Association for the Advancement of Native American Arts and Crafts, 1983.

Morgan, Lewis Henry. *League of the Iroquois.* Secaucus, N.J.: Citadel Press, 1962.

Sheppard, Sally. *Indians of the Eastern Woodlands.* New York: Franklin Watts, 1975.

INDEX

DATE DUE
